THE STORY OF CHRISTMAS

LADYBIRD BOOKS, INC.
Auburn, Maine 04210, USA.

© LADYBIRD BOOKS LTD 1993
Loughborough, Leicestershire, England.
Printed in Hong Kong

The Story of Christmas

Retold by Linda Jennings
with Illustrations by Gwen and Pat Tourret

A very long time ago, in a town called Nazareth, there lived a girl whose name was Mary.

One day Mary was out walking in the countryside when suddenly a bright, shining angel appeared.

"Don't be afraid," said the angel. "I am sent from God with a very special message. You will bear a son, and you shall call him Jesus. He will be the greatest king the world has ever known. He will be the Son of God."

Mary could hardly take in the amazing news. She was an ordinary village girl. How could she give birth to God's son? But she knew that God's word was the truth. "It is God's will," she said, bowing her head. "I am honored that He has chosen me."

ow Mary was engaged to a carpenter called Joseph. He, too, was visited by the angel.

"Mary's child is the Son of God," the angel told him. "Take Mary for your wife, and look after her well, for you will be the boy's father on Earth."

So Joseph married Mary and together the young couple looked forward to the birth of Jesus.

A few months later, it was ruled that every man in the kingdom must return to the town of his birth to sign a special register of names. Joseph and Mary had to make the long journey to Bethlehem in Judea. Mary's baby was nearly due, and Joseph was worried about her.

He saddled the donkey, and gently helped his wife onto its back. "We will find somewhere to rest as soon as we arrive," he promised Mary.

*T*he journey was a long one. By the time they reached Bethlehem, Mary was exhausted.

"We must find somewhere to stay," said Joseph. He and Mary walked from inn to inn, but every one of them was full.

"Have you nowhere my wife can sleep?" Joseph asked the last innkeeper in town. "She is expecting a baby."

The innkeeper raised his lantern to Mary's tired face. "There is room in my stable," he said. "Follow me."

*T*he stable was dark and filled with animals, but it was warm and dry. Joseph laid out his cloak on a bed of hay, and Mary sank down thankfully upon it. It was here, in the quietness of the stable, with the cattle breathing softly, that Mary gave birth to her child. She gazed at his tiny sleeping face in wonder.

On the hills outside Bethlehem shepherds were keeping watch over their sheep. The night was long and chill, and they sat huddled by their fire. Suddenly a light brighter than the brightest moon shone out in the sky. The shepherds fell to the ground in fear, shielding their eyes from the brilliant light.

"Do not be afraid," said a voice. "I have great news for you."

The shepherds looked up and saw an angel, his arms spread across the sky.

"Go to Bethlehem," the angel ordered. "In a stable you will find a baby whose birth has been promised for hundreds of years. He is the Son of God."

As the shepherds rose to their feet a great host of angels appeared, singing joyfully at the news of the wonderful birth.

The shepherds hurried through the dark streets of the sleeping town. There, just as the angel had said, was the stable, with a single bright star shining over it. Inside they found Joseph and Mary, with her tiny baby sleeping in her arms. Could this be the Son of God? The shepherds stood in wonder, gazing down at the child. Then, one by one, they knelt to worship him.

ar away, in another country, three wise and learned men studied a bright new star in the sky.

"This star means the birth of a king," said one of the wise men, excitedly. "Come, we must travel to find him, for our ancient books tell us he will be the king of the Jews, and the greatest king of all time."

Without delay the wise men saddled their camels, chose precious gifts for the new young king, and traveled toward Judea, following the star that shone before them.

When the wise men reached the city of Jerusalem they called upon King Herod.

"We have heard of the birth of a new king," they said. "A bright star has guided us here."

Herod consulted his priests. He was told that the king of the Jews was to be born in the town of Bethlehem. "So it is written by the prophets," said the priests.

"When you have found this king, come back and tell me," Herod said to the wise men. "Then I shall also go to Bethlehem to worship him." The wise men bowed to King Herod, and went on their way.

Soon the wise men came, as the shepherds had before them, to the stable where Jesus lay. Mary and Joseph looked up in astonishment at the sight of the strangers dressed in fine clothes. One by one the wise men knelt and offered their gifts, caskets of gold and frankincense and myrrh. Mary touched her child's soft cheek. How wonderful that little Jesus, born in a simple stable, should be visited by such grand folk!

ow the wise men planned to return to Jerusalem to tell Herod where the young king of the Jews could be found, but that night they were visited by an angel.

"Go home another way," said the angel. "Herod plans to kill the young king because he is afraid of his power." So the wise men followed the angel's advice and went home by a different route. Herod was furious that the three wise men did not return to him. And since he did not know exactly where the baby king could be found, he ordered that every child in Bethlehem under the age of two be killed.

*T*hat night Joseph shook Mary awake. "Hurry," he said. "King Herod plans to send soldiers to Bethlehem to kill our son. An angel has told me that we must escape to Egypt."

They quickly gathered up their few belongings, saddled their donkey, and crept quietly from the sleeping town. When, next morning, Herod's soldiers arrived to carry out their terrible deed, the baby Jesus was far away and safe.

$\mathcal{A}$ few years later Herod died, and Joseph was able to bring his family back from Egypt to their own home in Nazareth. There the young Jesus grew up, a carpenter's son, until, as a man, he became Savior of the world.